MY ITALIAN HERITAGE

To order additional copies of this book, contact:

Xlibris

1-888-795-4274

www.Xlibris.com

Orders@Xlibris.com

Barbara Feltquate photograph by Al Churilla

ISBN: Softcover   978-1-7960-7924-1

            Hardcover   978-1-7960-7925-8

            EBook   978-1-7960-7923-4

Library of Congress Control Number: 2019920899

Print information available on the last page

Rev. date: 03/02/2020

DEDICATED
TO MY PARENTS

Sam and Ethel Amato

ITALIAN FLAG

A tricolor band of
green, red, and white
Waving freely a
magnificent sight
It has evolved throughout
Italian history
Displaying unification
of our nationality

MT. ETNA

A volcano on the island of Sicily
At the summit view the emerald sea
What a beautiful and mesmerizing sight
When it is active and glows into the night

ITALY

Our forefathers came from a foreign land
With hills and dales and cliffs so grand
Architecture that takes your breath away
Old spiraling churches that still stand today
Home of scientists, artists, and writers galore
Food, fashion, music, and so much more

SICILY

A southerly island
and region of Italy
Wonderfully unique
and steeped in history
A land of important
and ancient sights
Captured by countries
proving their might
Many governments
influenced their identity
Signs of civilization
date back to 3000 BC

LEONARDO DA VINCI

Born in Florence,
Italy, in 1452
He accomplished
what he set out to do
A skilled scientist,
sculptor, and engineer
His works of art are
known everywhere
He painted *Mona Lisa*
and *The Last Supper* too
They hang in museums
for the public to view

MICHELANGELO

The best-known artist of the sixteenth century
He sculptured marble from a stone quarry
Most famous for the *Pieta* and the *David* statue
The dome of St. Peter's Basilica, his design too
His Sistine Chapel fresco is really divine
He lived to the impressive age of eighty-nine

AMERIGO VESPUCCI

An Italian merchant and navigator
Set sail from Spain lands to explore
Some say it was based on a whim
That America was named after him

GONDOLA

A traditional
Venetian watercraft
Long and narrow
and painted black
Used to sail across
the waterway
The best means to
travel in Venice today

GONDOLIER

The oarsman that captains an elongated boat
Skillfully navigating to stay afloat
Serenading his passengers, mister and miss
As the happy couple steal a sweet kiss

LEANING TOWER OF PISA

A tower that took two
hundred years to build
When the soft ground
broke, it started to tilt
To preserve the medieval
heritage of the town
Ongoing restorations save
it from falling down

COLOSSEUM

An architectural wonder built in 70 AD
Ruins still stand in Rome for all to see
The largest open-air oval amphitheater
Spectators watch the battling gladiator
Fifty thousand or more viewed in delight
As man or animal put up a fierce fight

THE VATICAN

A walled district in the city of Rome
Where the Pope lives and calls his home
An independent state and principality
The center of Roman Catholic Christianity

ST. PETER'S BASILICA

A magnificent church in St. Peter's Square
Worshippers travel from far and near
To watch the Pope from his balcony
Bless the worldwide community

IL PAPA/THE POPE

The Roman Catholic leader is the Pope
He offers us inspiration and hope
In matters of faith and morality
His guidance is the highest authority

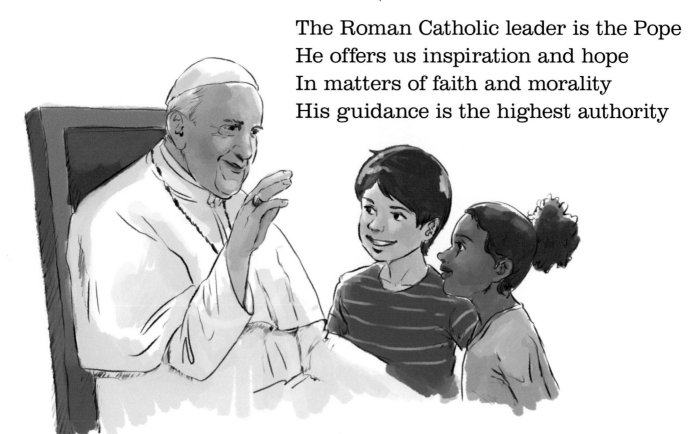

SAINT FRANCIS OF ASSISI

Most beloved
patron saint of Italy
Lived a humble
life of poverty
His prayers
inspired peace
and love
In a voice as
gentle as a dove

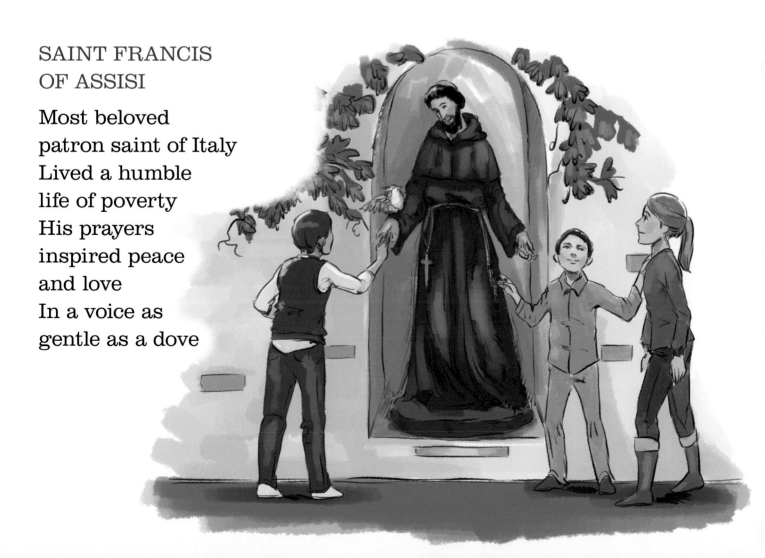

CHRISTMAS

A celebration of Christ's birth
That brings peace to those on earth
A time to spread joy and happiness
Is the truest meaning of Christmas

JESUS

The central figure in Christianity
Caring and loving to humanity
A redeemer who atoned for our sins
Offering forgiveness from within
He was crucified on Good Friday
And resurrected on Easter Sunday

THE FEAST OF THE SEVEN FISHES

A Christmas Eve tradition in an Italian home
Celebrated from Sicily all the way to Rome
Platters of eel and a cod called *baccala*
Smelt, calamari and red lobsters from afar
Mussels and shrimp such a wonderful treat
Makes up for the fact we cannot eat meat

EASTER

An important Christian holiday
Celebrated in a very special way
Some march the streets in
a solemn procession
In church, we remember
Christ's resurrection
We enjoy foods symbolic
of life and tasty to eat
Like painted eggs, ham,
and bread of wheat

ITALIANS

Proud and passionate people who live in Italy
Take joy and delight in friends and family
Known for being exuberant or head strong
When the mood arises, may burst into song
They respect old ways, customs, and tradition
Preserving our heritage is their mission

IL NONNO

My Italian grandfather is called *Nonno*
He gardens and watches his plants grow
Into the best tomatoes, squash, and beans
Fertilized by the fish from the stream
He tells stories about Italian folklore
We sit on his lap and ask for more

LA NONNA

Grandmother in Italian is called *Nonna*
Her kitchen smells of garlic and steamy pasta
She radiates warmth, wisdom, and grace
In a home that is the gathering place
Her life revolves around the family
With pictures on walls for all to see
In an honest and straight forward way
She gives good advice on living each day

LA FAMIGLIA/THE FAMILY

The most important part of an Italian's life
Where support is found in times of strife
Generations remain close and connected
Respect and love of the elderly is protected
On Sundays, we gather from far and near
For that pasta dinner we hold so dear

FOOD OF THE LAND

Italians love to
cook and eat
Hard crusty bread,
pasta, or meat
When picked ripe
from the vine
Grapes at harvest
turn into wine
Sunflowers flourish
in the rich soil
Producing the
country's olive oil

PUSHCART

A wooden wagon
built to display
Fruits and
vegetables on
market day
Stacks of
sausages, pork,
and veal
Fresh caught
tuna, squid, or eel
Arrange your
wares favorably
For a quick sale,
one, two, three!

PASTA

A food found in every Italian kitchen
Served with gravy, cheese, or chicken
Years ago, it was called spaghetti
When *al dente*, it was ready
Now in shapes large and small
Still best in red sauce and meatball

PIZZA

Modern pizza was created in the eighteenth century
In honor of Queen Margherita of Naples, Italy
Italian immigrants brought it to the USA
A most popular food in our country today

CANNOLI

An Italian pastry originating in Sicily
With a creamy filling mixed skillfully
Stuff a tube shell with ricotta cheese
Top with nuts, may I have another, please

BISCOTTI

A crispy cookie that is baked twice
With almonds and anise in every slice
Dip it in coffee or a glass of milk
It melts in your mouth just like silk

GELATO

The Italian word for ice cream
Sweet as a heavenly dream
Stack it high on a waffle cone
Or serve in a bowl all alone

FRUIT, CHEESE, AND NUTS

Italians frequently complete a meal
With a cheese wedge or an orange to peel
Crack open a hard shelled nut or two
A favorite way to satisfy me or you

SOCCER

Referred to as football outside the USA
The most popular sport in the world today
To Italians, their soccer league is grand
Bringing passion and pride to the land

TARANTELLA

An Italian folk dance
with a lively beat
Clap your hands
and kick your feet
Twirl your partner
round and round
Hold on tight so
you don't fall down

BOCCE

A bowling game
Italian style
Where young and
old idle awhile
A sport that dates
back to 5000 BC
We still outwit our
opponent gleefully
Played on sand
packed really hard
Or on grass in your
own backyard

PINOCCHIO

A story of a marionette
carved from wood
With misadventures on
his road to be good
It tells of faith and
love of family
Importance of truth
and generosity
The consequences
of a lie or deceit
His nose grows, almost
touching his feet
Goodness is rewarded
with ultimate joy
At journey's end, he
becomes a real boy

BUONGIORNO

A greeting and special wish for you
To have a good day whatever you do
Tip your hat in a fond and cordial salute
Have a sweet day like a bowl of fruit

GRAZIE AND PER FAVORE

Grazie for thank you, *per favore* for please
Kind words spoken graciously with ease
Good manners are important in society
Showing respect, care, and courtesy

CIAO

An Italian word adopted across the seas
In the United States and other countries
Originated in Latin as "How can I serve you?"
Now it's a friendly goodbye or "How do you do?"

ACKNOWLEDGEMENTS

As always, to my dear husband Harvey and my beloved family; Debbie and Glenn, David and Anne, and grandchildren Brad, Alex, Ethan, and Jakob. You are all my inspiration and greatest treasure. My wonderful sister, Janet Miller and dear friend Pam Susidko whose artistic abilities and imaginations lovingly made suggestions and kept me on track. A wholehearted thank you to the Churilla clan. Al Churilla, my amazing photographer and his lovely wife and my dear friend, Sherry whose support has been ongoing. Mike Churilla my genealogy guru and Juanita Churilla whose early childhood development teaching skills made sure that it would be an interactive book between reader and child. To my Cape Cod friends Mary Sullivan and Diane Kenney for their enthusiasm and encouragement. To Ron and Liz Eckert who suggested that the illustrations be in Line Drawing format with splashes of vibrant color. You all contributed your talents in a unique manner and I am deeply grateful.

Printed in the United States
By Bookmasters